I0796642

MUSICAL INSTRUMENTS

Maria Koran

EYEDISCOVER

Go to www.eyediscover.com and enter this book's unique code.

BOOK CODE

AVS68643

EYEDISCOVER brings you optic readalongs that support active learning.

Published by AV² by Weigl
350 5th Avenue, 59th Floor New York, NY 10118
Website: www.eyediscover.com

Library of Congress Cataloging-in-Publication Data available on request

ISBN 978-1-7911-0778-9 (hardcover)

Printed in Guangzhou, China
1 2 3 4 5 6 7 8 9 0 23 22 21 20 19

072019
121818

Project Coordinator: John Willis
Designer: Mandy Christiansen and Ana Maria Vidal

Weigl acknowledges Alamy, Getty Images, iStock, and Shutterstock as the primary image suppliers for this title.

EYEDISCOVER provides enriched content, optimized for tablet use, that supplements and complements this book. EYEDISCOVER books strive to create inspired learning and engage young minds in a total learning experience.

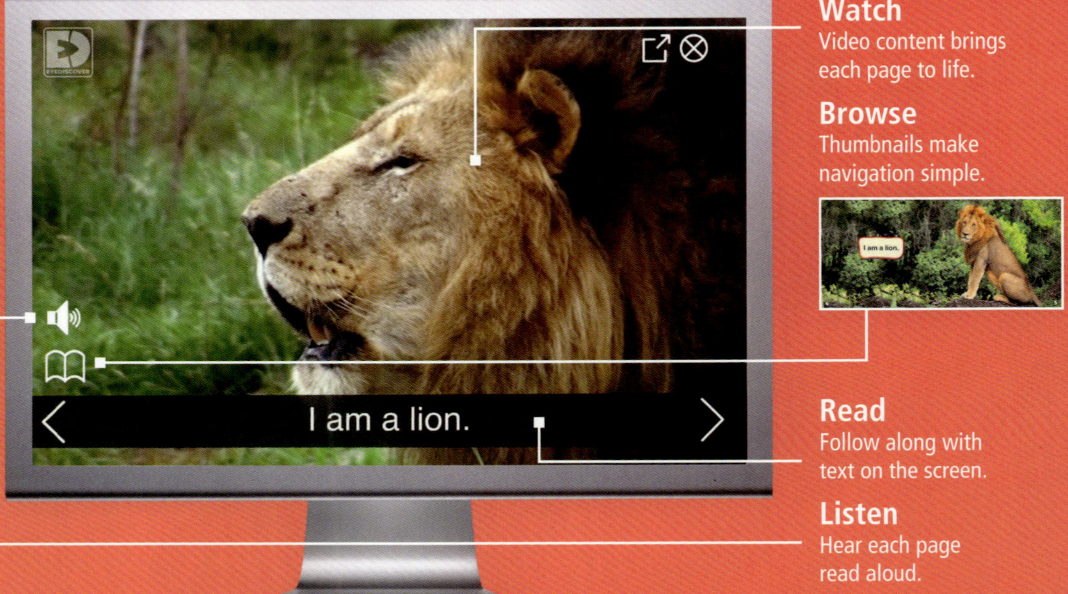

Your EYEDISCOVER Optic Readalongs come alive with...

Audio
Listen to the entire book read aloud.

Video
High resolution videos turn each spread into an optic readalong.

OPTIMIZED FOR

- TABLETS
- WHITEBOARDS
- COMPUTERS
- AND MUCH MORE!

MUSICAL INSTRUMENTS

In this book, you will learn about

- what they are called
- what they look like
- how they are played

and much more!

A musical instrument is used to make music. People play a piano by pushing its keys.

Keyboards are smaller than pianos. Some keyboards can sound like other kinds of instruments.

People play drums by hitting them with drumsticks or their hands.

Guitars are stringed instruments. A person can make music by plucking a guitar's strings.

Violins are another kind of stringed instrument. To play the violin, a person pulls a bow across its strings.

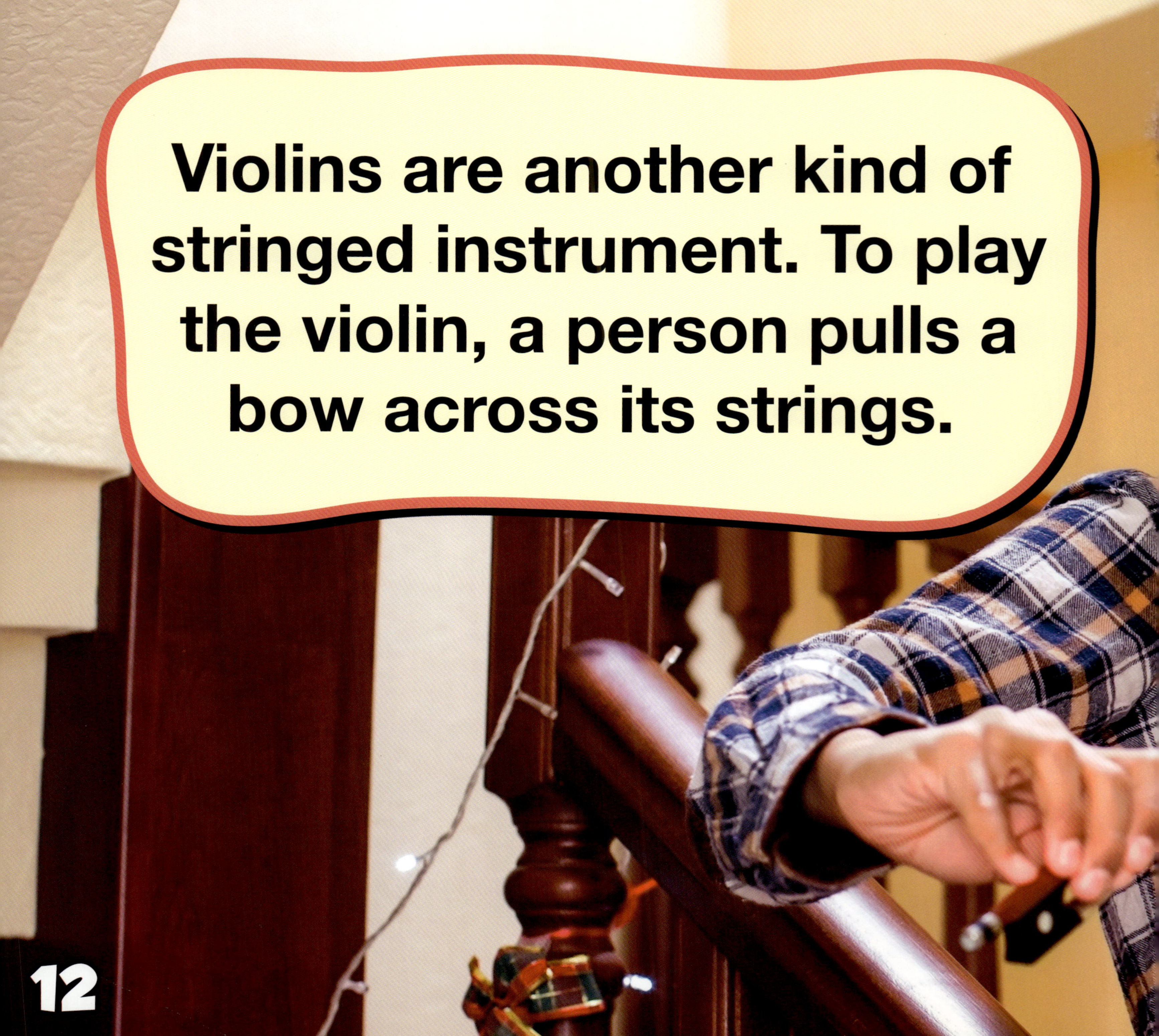

Cellos look like large violins. People need to sit down to play these instruments.

Trumpets are brass instruments. People blow into them and push down their keys.

A saxophone is shaped like the letter "J." The saxophone is a popular instrument in jazz music.

Flutes are some of the oldest musical instruments on Earth. They come in many different sizes.

MUSICAL INSTRUMENTS BY THE NUMBERS

A piano has **88 keys**.

Violins were **first made** about **500 years** ago.

Most **guitars** have six strings.

People have been playing **drums** for at least **7,500 years**.

Most **Saxophones** have 24 **holes**.

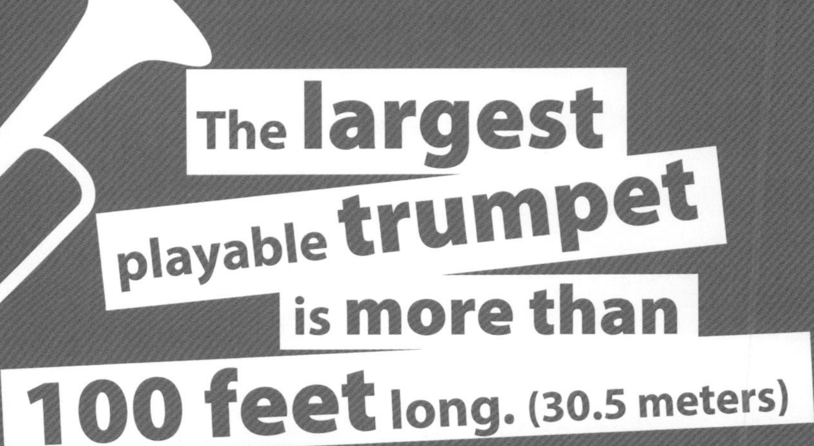

The **largest** playable **trumpet** is **more than** **100 feet** long. (30.5 meters)

KEY WORDS

Research has shown that as much as 65 percent of all written material published in English is made up of 300 words. These 300 words cannot be taught using pictures or learned by sounding them out. They must be recognized by sight. This book contains 40 common sight words to help young readers improve their reading fluency and comprehension. This book also teaches young readers several important content words, such as proper nouns. These words are paired with pictures to aid in learning and improve understanding.

Page	Sight Words First Appearance
4	a, by, is, its, make, people, play, to, used
7	are, can, kinds, like, of, other, some, sound, than
8	hands, or, their, them, with
12	another, the
15	down, large, look, need, these
16	and, into
18	in, letter
21	come, different, Earth, many, on, they

Page	Content Words First Appearance
4	keys, music, musical instrument, piano
7	keyboards
8	drums, drumsticks
11	guitars, strings
12	bow, violins
15	cellos
16	trumpets
18	jazz music, saxophone
21	flutes, sizes

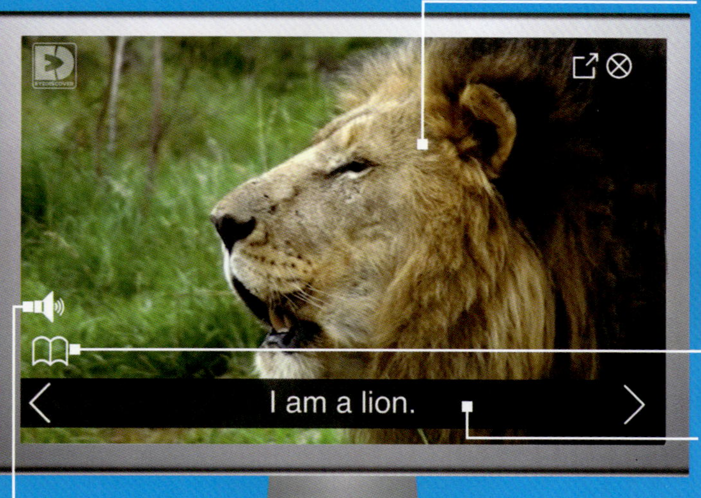

Watch
Video content brings each page to life.

Browse
Thumbnails make navigation simple.

Read
Follow along with text on the screen.

Listen
Hear each page read aloud.

Go to www.eyediscover.com and enter this book's unique code.

BOOK CODE

AVS68643